The Long Road Home

poems by

Martin Lammon

Finishing Line Press
Georgetown, Kentucky

The Long Road Home

Copyright © 2020 by Martin Lammon
ISBN 978-1-64662-178-1 First Edition
All rights reserved under International and Pan-American Copyright Conventions. No part of this book may be reproduced in any manner whatsoever without written permission from the publisher, except in the case of brief quotations embodied in critical articles and reviews.

Publisher: Leah Maines

Editor: Christen Kincaid

Cover Art: Pexels, Pixabay.com

Author Photo: Martin Lammon

Cover Design: Martin Lammon

Printed in the USA on acid-free paper.
Order online: www.finishinglinepress.com
also available on amazon.com

Author inquiries and mail orders:
Finishing Line Press
P. O. Box 1626
Georgetown, Kentucky 40324
U. S. A.

Table of Contents

Back Roads

Between the Numbers 1
Searching for Emus 2
Feeding Pigs 3
1969 5
Bird Offering 6
The Only Other Beautiful Thing 8
From a Back Alley Balcony in Tuscany, I See Dante's Starlings 9
The Bird I Would Be 10
Back Roads 11
I Snore 13

The Road Not Taken

How Like a Son 17
Killing Pigs 18
A Fable: Why the Village Will Never Be Empty 20
Lost Lesson from Japanese Children's Class on Shushin 22
My Sister Tells Me Her Prayer for the World of Men 23
XY 24
Sestina Qué Triste 25
In Cortona, Walking Beside a Wall Erected Before Christ,
    I Contemplate Longing 27
Poetry Fathers 28
What Goats Know 30
Home Run 31
Glory Days 33
Zigzag 34

At the End of the Open Road

Sons and Fathers 37
Blood Mountain Villanelle 38
The Birds are Dying and Singing 39
Help 40
The Day of the Eclipse, My Mother Is Almost Herself Again 41
The Holy Land 43

Anno Domini 2004 44
Commandments 45
Come Back 46
Obituary 47
A Romance 48
My Wife and I Learn to Accept Our Clutter 49

Notes 51

Acknowledgements 53

Bio 55

For my mother and father, brother and sister

and for my wife, Libby

Back Roads

I began in Ohio.
I still dream of home.

—"Stages of a Journey Westward," James Wright
From *The Branch Will Not Break* (1963)

Between the Numbers

>...even before returning from the hospital, a new baby
represents an outlay of roughly $450 in medical expenses.
>
>—*Life*, June 16, 1958

The year I was born, *Life*
cost twenty-five cents,
two bits those days, a chunk of change.

Back then my father wore a hat
to church, oiled his hair with *Vitalis*.
That summer, he gave up baseball, painted houses,
washed his hands with turpentine. That was the year
his wife turned twenty, he turned twenty-one.
The year I got my father's scent.

According to my Baby Book,
I cost one hundred two dollars
and thirty-five cents, a fortune for my father
who promised Clinton County Hospital
he'd pay twelve dollars a month.

That was the year of diapers, powders and creams.
The year my father started paying on time.
The year a man got the first quick whiff
what his nine-pounds, four-ounces added up to,
his handful, his bundle, his secret stash.

Searching for Emus

> I can, with one eye squinted, take it all as a blessing.
>
> —Flannery O'Connor, letter to Elizabeth and Robert Lowell, March 17, 1953

Sunrise, I search for emus lurking near
the magnolia tree. It's true, a good emu's hard to find.

Last week, the local TV News interviewed eyewitnesses
who swore they saw giant birds crossing the Old Sparta Road,
cutting through neighbors' backyards. Then the story broke,
how a Baldwin County man admitted he'd unleashed
three breeding pairs. *Let'em forage*, he said, *there's miles of creeks
and woods*—his homestead lay near the Oconee River—
Give'em a year, no more'n two, the hunt'll be on.

In Milledgeville, Georgia, perhaps
all that fellow saw was a flightless bird, dull-
colored, plain ugly, plumb lucky
for a thousand acres, nothing so fancy
as Flannery's peacocks, those storied,
iridescent birds, regal and aloof.

A better man might've been suspicious
about a bird could look him in the eye.
He might've surfed that World Wide Web,
landed himself in Australia, where seventy thousand emus
migrate, rooting for foliage. He might've clicked on Aussie farmers,
plucky and desperate, erecting a fence six hundred miles long.

A better man might've known it's emu males that nest
and hatch a brood's chicks, how the flock will pause,
and female emus will linger, while hunter green eggs
incubate beneath the male's humble body.

A better man might've taken the time to learn something,
might've watched anxious females scratch the dirt,
like no proud peacock, nor good old Baldwin County boy
whose spilled blood's the color of this land he cleaves to.

Feeding Pigs

Back when I was just a boy,
I watched my grandmother gathering slop,
kitchen peelings, a feast fit for hungry pigs:
potatoes, carrots, apples, tomatoes,
rhubarb, cucumbers, pea pods, egg shells.
"Pigs'll eat most anything," she said,
"even a boy's fingers he hain't careful."

Harvests, our husked field corn hardened to stone.
I remember the iron shelling machine, my father
cranking the handle. I tossed in a corn cob, and kernels
flowed down a spout like pearls into our metal pail.

*

We fed pigs slop and corn, and I watched
the way their snouts would root and sniff
as if smell mattered most to a hog.
I remember one cold Ohio morning,
my uncle and I shoveled mud and pig shit
three inches deep. My dad's baby brother, thirteen
and mean as any boy could be, teased
he'd feed me to them hungry pigs.

"Bet you'd taste better'n old kitchen slop,"
he said, hoisting me over the fence, hogs
squealing like they'd caught the scent of me.

*

One day after church, I pedaled my bike
to the graveyard on the hill near our family farm.
Staring at headstones, I sounded out names.
Even back then, I could read and figure, subtract years
between death-dates and birth-dates.

I remember rubbing my fingers

over smooth granite, the empty spaces left
for the living. Even back then, I knew
everyone died: my grandfather, his hogs
fattened before the slaughter, someday
my father, my mother, even a boy like me,

who dreamed of getting even with
his monstrous uncle, no matter how
colossal he was, how ferocious,
how mortal.

1969

They don't feel pain, my father said.
In my right hand, I squeezed the bluegill
behind its head, wrapped my palm over
the dorsal fin, folded back fishbone spines
like a Chinese paper fan. In my left hand,
my strong hand, I pinched the hook
the way my father taught me.
I pulled the barb through lip
and gum. I heard a rip like rags tearing.

Nineteen sixty-nine, eleven years old,
what did I know about keeping fish
breathing as long as they could? My father
threaded their gills with a nylon cord, our day's
catch like charms on a bracelet, dangling
in the water beside our boat.

Back home, after fishing, my father
handed me the scaling knife. I cut off
heads and tails, I scraped scales, I gutted blue gill
or perch we'd deep fry for supper or freeze
for later. Those days, we stored filleted fish
beside icy bags of sweet corn, lima beans, peas,
our summer vegetables persisting through winter.

Back then, what did I know about keeping bodies fresh
from air and rot? What did I know about growing a garden,
feeding a family, filling a freezer with bluegill and perch?
What did I know about those boys on the news
zipped up, stacked in plastic bags, airtight and waterproof?

Bird Offering

Spring again, and birds are building a nest, again,
inside our garage. Bird shit splatters our cars,
and finally, when my wife is out of town,
I find a pole to knock the nest down.

But first I pound the high ledge, probing
for a lingering bird. I listen, hear nothing.
Not one chirp, no rustling pine straw.
It's empty, I think, perhaps I'll find
a hollow egg or two, so I sweep
my long pole side to side, pry
loose the nest's dried mud and grass,
until everything gives, falls,

and two birds tumble out, their wings flailing
against falling, as if ruffled birds, almost aloft,
might still fly. Instead, their bodies flutter and wobble
just urgently enough to break their fall, and I know
they are not dead, and that they are.

                                              I find a broom,
sweep the nestlings out, their wing-stubs flapping
against my sweeping. I roll them over the driveway
and into our woods nearby. Among dead leaves,
their tiny bodies ball up and hunker down.

*

What else would instinct have them do?
What else could I have done, I'd plead to my wife
if she were here—layer a shoebox with moss? Dig up worms,
mash them into paste? Add water, pretend an eyedropper
was a mother's beak, play nursemaid to foundlings?

Early next morning, I find the world
I knew I'd find, empty, newborn birds
no match for an owl, an easy snatch for feral cats.

*

Two weeks later, my wife's back home,
and somehow the nest's returned, as if our birds, longing
for mating, their will unflappable, have dared
to test my nerve. I tell my wife nothing,
knock the new nest down, and if the story ended there,
I might scratch out "their will," write "instinct" as before.

But the next day I walk outside,
and atop a brick wall beside our garage
I find an egg the size of a jelly bean.
And when I lift it to the light, the shell,
translucent, reveals a yolk, the dark speck
of an embryonic eye, and there's no logic

can deny it's a bird's impossible egg, gently laid
upon a brick wall, as if I've been offered an even trade
or outright bribe. So I carry the egg inside,
show it to my wife, tell her the whole story.

The look she gives me, I've seen before,
and for a moment, what willfulness ravels
anew in me, what world, whose world, unravels?
Long-married and alone, we take turns swapping
the egg back and forth as if we're afraid
what will hatch, unbidden and unbearable.

The Only Other Beautiful Thing

After the long summer, I close the windows,
and I think about a woman I knew, who once
walked out of the hot shower
with a towel on her head, nothing more,
and when she dressed, she didn't put on
clothes the way most of us do. No, instead
she stood there naked, put on her shoes first,
high-heeled Italian shoes. If any other woman
I knew had put on her shoes first, I'd have laughed,
but she was so beautiful, especially
with a towel on her head, and shoes
from Italy on her feet.

The only other beautiful thing
that cold night in November
was a brown moth big as my thumb
that I caught in my hand
and held there, wings thrumming
against my palm as if its whole body
were a tiny feathered heart.

From a Back Alley Balcony in Tuscany, I See Dante's Starlings

They swipe the sky, Dante's
starlings, they dip and zag,
they tear the air like Furies.

Fork-tailed, white-bellied birds,
spiriti mali, they scream and scatter
as if possessed, as if the wind
roiled their wings, as if
their feathers were fins.

A blur, a flock of souls
aflame, lusty, hungry—
like a clutch of piranha, like a hive of bees,
like a fugue of fugitive apparitions,
their flight like needlepoints of light.

The Bird I Would Be

The ocean heron high-steps
in shallow waters, bobs
and weaves like a boxer
afraid to take a punch,
rubbernecks and stalks
minnows at low tide.

Pelicans survey dunes,
flap wings, wait, and wait,
then flap again. They convoy
like old B-52 bombers. At sea
one pelican breaks ranks, strafes
the tips of ocean waves for fish.

Off shore, not far, the gull
hovers, then plummets
like an angler's lead sinker.
The bird splashes, submerges,
then shakes itself out
of the water, flies away hungry.

When old crow finds a beached
apple core, he twists his thick neck
left, right, then just like me, panics
when the surf rears up.

Crow hops and beats wings, exactly like
a crow, the high ground ever close-by.

Back Roads

Near Wauseon, Ohio, my father drives
his father from Ottokee to Tedrow,
across Bean Creek to Fayette, that town
where my mother was born. These flat lands

fool my father. The gridwork of roads, tilled
fields, and abandoned railroad lines
crisscross Fulton county. He hasn't lived here
since before I was born. Now his father has forgotten

how keys work, how this one starts the car,
how another slides open the deadbolt. The old
man has forgotten his son's name. But if a body,
mind, and soul are one and knit together one life,

what thread unravels when a man can't tie his shoelaces
or button his shirt? Where's the soul gone when honey,
salt, and dill taste the same? My father's
father stares out the car window. Years ago,

they sold eggs in Wauseon and Maumee,
kept cows, raised hogs, planted corn. They plowed
the Ohio Turnpike that stripped the land west
of Toledo. Now my father is lost, steers

by instinct. He knows that, soon, he'll have to
give up, pull over and ask some stranger for help.

*

After my grandfather has died, my father phones me
in Georgia, tells this story, about back roads

I'd never find on a map. He tells me
how his father said "Turn here," pointing
east, then said "turn," and again, "turn,"
past old farms, ruined barns, all the way home.

My father goes silent, and I know
he tells me this story because he cannot say
how he is proud, how he's waited fifty years
for this saga about his father, that last

crisis where adrenalin surges and the heart's
ventricle squeezes blood to the brain, and fathers
shed fear and shame like an old skin, tell their lost
sons "here, turn here." And if my father and I

cannot say where the soul goes when we die, or if
we have souls, what we have is enough. I have
his nose, his big thighs. My body, older now,
will make a good fit for his discarded skin.

I Snore

> The secret
> Of this journey is to let the wind
> Blow its dust all over your body,
> To let it go on blowing, to step lightly, lightly
> All the way through your ruins, and not to lose
> Any sleep over the dead, who surely
> Will bury their own, don't worry.
>
> —*James Wright, "The Journey"*

My wife swears I snore
like a foghorn, and she's not the first
drowsy woman I've shocked awake,
but she's the one who's stuck with me,
who endures my sonorous nocturnes, my epic
sagas that would raise the dead.

Listen, newlyweds or twice-divorced,
hot shot millennials, or even old-hands like me,
before it's too late, let us forgive a lover's addiction
to moisturizing lip gloss, late-night noshing,
or endless channel surfing. Celebrate your honey's
fondness for mocha java chip, and overlook your muffin's
boring bimbo fantasies. Let us embrace whatever foibles we can,
unleash what we can't. Let's strap on leather or lace and raise
a holy ruckus, or let us snore like foghorns, but tonight let's not
lose any sleep over the dead, who surely will bury their own, don't worry.
Let's snatch one deep breath, live light as a feather and as long as we can,
and for once let us all get a good night's sleep.

The Road Not Taken

How Like a Son

Ten years old, I listened to my mother's
story, how a woman, a stranger, had shifted
gears in a hurry, backed over her son, braked,
panicked, shifted again, jerked forward.
Her boy was twice-crushed. His mother
screamed. My father tried to help.
My mother told me never to tell.

But when I heard this story, how I wanted
to be that boy, look into my father's eyes
and believe he could save me, to tell everyone
he'd held on to my life as if it were his own.

How like a son to heap more death
on his father. How like a boy
to hoist a man up, hang him high,
and years later, wonder why
the old man's so aloof, or why
his body sways, then slows
like Grandpa's cuckoo clock,
its long pendulum
winding down.

Killing Pigs

> Donna Deason is having a problem with wild hogs digging up her yard. She has spoken with the game warden and he has approved having them killed. If you are interested in killing these pigs, please get in touch with Donna at Baskin Robbins. These pigs range in size from baby pigs to grown pigs.
>
> —University email

One woman wonders out loud which of these pigs
teaches in our department. One man warns,
beware October's flavor-of-the-month.
How can we resist? We were trained in irony.
We eye each other sidewise, wonder ourselves
who secretly longs to cross over the semantic gap
between *having them killed* and *killing these pigs*.

*

China domesticated hogs
nine thousand years ago. Columbus
and *conquistadores* brought pigs
to the Americas—today's feral razorback,
cloven-hooved, enlarged canines
curling out each jaw. "Tusks," we say,
just one gene we tinker with. We breed
Berkshire, Yorkshire, Chester White,
Duroc, Hampshire, Poland China,
Landrace and Spotted hogs, fine names
for thin-skinned, tusk-less swine.

In Middle Georgia, after the long War, forsaken
pigs scavenged the Oconee River's flood plain
for yams, grubs, plump black raspberries. No barn
or sty was fit for them, no smokehouse,
no penned wallow. Those lost hogs bred,
and now their wild progeny's loose
and rooting up a woman's lawn.

*

Donna Deason, I sympathize. Years ago, in Ohio's
Athens County, I watched nine infant marmots
emerge from their winter den below the porch
and gnaw on the grass outside my kitchen door. Each pup
was harmless, the size of my hand, all nine together
nothing so fierce as a feral hog. Yet when I threw open
the door, hooted and hollered, all but one scattered.

Later, I read in a book how the brood's oldest stands guard.
But by then I'd seen for myself how a marmot pup's hiss and teeth
are fearsome enough if you're a bare-legged man
shivering half-naked in your morning robe.

If you're from Ohio or Georgia, you call them woodchucks,
or groundhogs. The name doesn't matter. Gardens are ravaged.

I couldn't kill them, Donna, but had it done. One day,
when I was out of town, my landlord farmer and his son
lay down in tall grass thirty yards off, rifles ready,
and one by one, each pup surely exploded.

Donna, I couldn't even watch my groundhogs being slaughtered,
how those two determined, keen-eyed men took aim and killed
that litter of half-pigs without malice, wit, or irony.

A Fable: Why the Village Will Never Be Empty

Once a year, the old story goes,
elders turn their backs on the village
and start walking towards the Great Mountain
seeking a quiet place to recite a poem or sing a song
no one else may ever hear, not even a beloved
wife or husband, not even a favorite niece or nephew.

One man may grieve for his grandfather, who died
before he taught his sons how to dance, how to sing
before the hunt, and after. How to slaughter,
how not to slaughter, and how men laugh
with their wives, and with other men. One woman
may lean beside the tree where her mother told the tale
of the lucky bride's forehead marked with God's thumbprint,
and she prays her own daughter will never settle for less
than love. All afternoon, these voices swarm
like bees ecstatic for mountain flowers.

If you love your verses, you write them down, wrap them
in broad leaves. You carry your words
up the mountain, as high as you can
and still catch your breath.

There, you set your words on fire, watch the smoke
rise, and lift up your voice. If you please God,
then you may hear ice melting, or a salamander breathing,
some sure sign, and you'll never leave the mountaintop.

Or all is silent. You climb down,
return to the village, find your sleepy husband
or tireless wife. You live a long life
never knowing the mountain's holiness
of bare rock, God's pure and empty altitude.

Years later, you'll die in your sleep, the way
your father said he wanted to go.

You know what comes next. Or you'll never know.

Lost Lesson from Japanese Children's Class on *Shushin*

One hundred years ago
how dark was Omasu's
shame? Daughter
of a man on trial for theft,
fifteen years old and terrified
to testify, she bit her tongue

off. Blood poured from
her mouth, her hot, flushed
face at last going pale
and serene. She was so beautiful
and admirable, a rich man
married her and took care of her

father, found innocent, a man revered
in his village for having such a daughter
who would never say a word
against elder or husband.

My Sister Tells Me Her Prayer for the World of Men

Lord, let my body no longer betray me.
Lord, let me be transparent.
Let a man unburden and confess
he's waited for me his whole life.

Lord, let me welcome a husband
home from work. Let us sit together
on the couch, turn off the TV.
Lord, let us be quiet.

In bed, in the dark, Lord, let my husband
hold me and for once let a man know
the difference between his body and mine.

XY

The other side of blunt
        is brute

The other side of blush
        is beard

The other side of weird
        is wired

The other side of suck
        is suckle

The other side of nipple
        is nipple

The other side of me
        is she and he

Their bruised blood is plum
        the other side of pink

Sestina Qué Triste

Say *la piedra.*
What pity
In a stone? Loss,
Perhaps, *no más,*
No menos. Squint, you miss
La ultima luz.

Say *la luz.*
Say *la piedra.*
In this language, pity
Abounds, and loss
Is common. We chant *una más*
As if we might miss

The saddest song, or miss
Una punta de la luz
So small, *una piedra*
So smooth, we will pity
Each other as if such loss
Were *triste. Qué más,*

Qué más? Mucho más
Y mucho menos. I miss
Nuance, say *luz*
When I mean *la raza*, say *piedra*
When I mean *pebble.* A pity,
This meaning I've lost.

We live with loss
Y queremos más,
Want what we miss
Most. At night, *la luz;*
In flight, *la piedra,*
Tierra firma. Want pity

When we have no pity.
In this *milagro* of language, loss

Lingers on the tongue, *más*
O menos, and I miss
La playa, la lengua de la costa, la luz
En la mañana. I say *piedra*

As if I'd said *pity.* Say *luz*
As if I'd said *loss.* Only a word, *una piedra,*
Such sad syllables, what I miss *la más.*

In Cortona, Walking Beside a Wall Erected Before Christ, I Contemplate Longing

If rivers were wine, if wine
were wounds, if wounds were stones—

If stones were olives, if olives
were sunlight, if sun were rain—

If rain were wind, if wind
were fire, if fire were bread—

If bread were blood, if blood
were poems, if poems were bone—

From bone, silence,
from silence, a vowel,

the scent of almonds,
almost a voice.

Poetry Fathers

We sit around the table, drinking and waiting
for dinner. I sip bourbon with James Wright
and I'm so damn happy to finally meet him.
"Tell me about those Indian ponies!" I say.
Robert Bly waves his hand as if to cast a spell.
He tells us how he wrenched the wheel away to make
Jim stop on such a goddamn cold day in Minnesota,
nearly seventy miles from home. Bob Pack
raises a finger, tells us home is nearer or farther,
is just so many miles away, but never *nearly* seventy.

Louis Simpson leans in, whispers in my ear, "Bull Shit."

Don Hall punches Bly in the ribs, launches lyrics about
the weather, how a dry fog circles the peak of Mount Kearsarge
in winter, or hovers in spring, ebullient, over Eagle Pond, so wet
and thick you wonder if a law of gravity's been broken.

Jim Dickey walks in, breaks a law of gravity, hauls
himself to the kitchen, stumbles out the back door.

Fatherly, Simpson pulls me closer, tells me to take time
for poems, for what matters. How the hell does he know
the dry spell I'm in, the silence I've settled into? I leave
the table for the men's room, look in the mirror. What wrinkles
give me away? What twitch or tick? But when I return

I find my fathers joined by *their* fathers! Erect and thin, T. S. Eliot,
teetotaler, fills Louis a tall glass with ice and scotch to the brim.
Off-key and sonorous, Pound sings in Hall's ear Alexandrine hymns
to Aeneas and Mussolini.

                        My poetry fathers squirm. They wish
their fathers would go away. And me? I couldn't be happier
to meet my grandfathers! Maybe they'll buy us spumoni ice cream,
tell stories about bespectacled Joyce, maudlin Yeats, or Hardy's
dark promise, how he said to hell with Judas critics and writing

angry novels, he'd write only poems instead—and he did—
and thirty years later, happy, he died.

                                        Then Old Ezra,
the man in white spats straightens up, stands, places
his hand on Don Hall's shoulder, sturdies himself,
and for one last lucid moment tests us all.

"How much did you lay down," he asks, "and when
were you all in?"
                        "All in," I boast, drunk and brave,
raising my glass, and the older men laugh, long and hard,
until it hurts them too much to laugh.

What Goats Know

Shall we quibble over sixty million years,
or even sixty thousand? Shall we argue with glaciers?
Who knows what slippery day the goat's kin first found
footing here, bred balance in their ruminant
progeny? The zoologist knows cloven hooves,
how the soft *subunguis* and hard *outer unguis*
cushion the goat's leap over boulders.
The poet gazes at Ha Ling Peak, overlooks
the goat, sees a brave man's face.

Ha Ling earned this mountain named for him.
Twice in one day, he conquered the lung-busting climb
and scrabble—once, to claim a white man's wager,
then again, to wave a flag, prove his stake, and collect.

But that hero's been dead a hundred years.
His whole life was less than a foot to the glacier,
was nothing to the ancient clan of mosquito
swarming this mountain valley each summer,
infamous to millennia of goats fleeing skyward.

Home Run

I've heard some say that *what goes up
must come down*. I wonder if that's true.
This year, I turned sixty-two, but even if I've lost
forty pounds, I'm not getting any younger.

Yet perhaps, when we die, we start over,
maybe our life clock rewinds. Maybe
we're born again as monkeys, pigs, or cows?
Perhaps we come back an Ayatollah, Dalai Lama,

a winged or wingless angel? Perhaps we ascend
to an enlightened consciousness, or simply dissolve
into molecules of carbon, hydrogen, those primordial
harbingers of life? *Presto*, we start all over again.

I've heard Newton's apple might not fall, might hang
suspended in mid-air, might even keep rising, higher,
higher, out of sight and out of mind, a quantum
coincidence, highly unlikely, but not impossible.

And what about the Reverend Billy Graham? I'd bet
good money his beliefs never faltered, even when Godless
naysayers assailed him. I'd bet the farm he'd swear
on his father's Bible his faith was ever buoyant.

And me? My favorite baseball team, year after year,
despite my fanatic faith, goes up and down. Ok, mostly down,
but damn if they don't surprise, start a winning streak, climb
up the standings, spin the fans around, win the pennant.

There was one slugger, a future Hall-of-Famer,
who hit a homerun so high, so far, it cleared the lights.
There's a statue where they say the ball landed
outside the stadium. But here's the lowdown,

the inside scoop: No one saw it touch down. They say
he swat that horsehide five hundred twenty feet,

but there's no witness, only that statue, a transparent
acrylic case, and inside, there's a scuffed-up ball.

But despite the immaculate view, I'm reminded
of Schrödinger's cat in a box, how maybe
it's there, maybe not. How *voilá*, the cat's dead,
or alive, or both. Or somewhere else.

How what you see is what you get
but never what you get to keep.

Glory Days

The baseball field is loose pebbles and dirt.
The bat is varnished hickory. The ball
is horsehide leather stitched with red thread.
The summer I turn twelve years old, the end
of Little League, the year before my body
sprouts hair and my father buys me a bottle
of *Old Spice*, I stare down the pitcher,
a big boy, who throws mean and inside.

Then just like that, ball and bat
make a noise like wood cracking
when an old tree falls, and I hold on,
squeeze that sound as long as I can,
the ball disappearing over the fence.

But no, it's years later, bedtime, and here I am
telling stories again. My wife pats my hand,
kisses my cheek. She rolls over, pulls back
the covers and turns off the light.

Who am I kidding? I'm still holding on,
deep-breathing, circling those bases, slowing
down for the long trot home.

Zigzag

Yes, I confess, I've zigged
when I should have zagged,
itched when I should have scratched.
I've lost count how often I've lied
when I should have lain, leaped
before I looked, and hung on
when I should have hanged. Once
I laughed so hard I thought I'd bust
a gut, burst into tears instead,
but that's another story, the old
cock-and-bull, how once a boy laughed
so hard he cried, lay down in his bed,
and wished he were dead, or dead certain,
just once, where his heart wanted to go.

Yes, I've cried myself asleep,
howled at blizzards, giggled the first time
a girl leaned down and touched me. I've jizzed
when I should have jazzed, I've laughed like crazy,
collapsed to my knees in tears, pounded
fists against the floor. I've fallen head over heels,
end over end, or like a man dead. I've fallen
like a flat stone skipped across a pond,
that finally slides into the deep water.

Yes, I confess, my *zaftig* heart heaves, swells,
and has heaped on me a world of trumped-up troubles,
blessings and blarney, infinite bliss and jest, has zigzagged
between zilch and zero, between the nothing under the bed
that terrorizes us, and the nothing we'll never know.

At the End of the Open Road

Sons and Fathers

Sons never listen when they're told
to sit still, take a breath, and hear
what fathers want their sons to know:

How to laugh at the boss's jokes.
How not to punch a wall. How to fight fair.
But boys don't listen when they're told

how to live their lives, least of all, when the old
man lies. Even worse, when he doesn't lie, shares
what he can, what he needs his sons to know.

Take my father. These days, he'd talk on the phone
all afternoon: stock prices, who's died, how my mother's
holding up. But do I listen? I'm told

slow down, enjoy growing old
with your wife. I tell him I'll do my best, I swear,
because I want to know what he needs me to know

more than I can say. So why am I again so slow
to tell him what he's waited so long to hear?
Why can't I listen, just this once, when I'm told
to listen?
                Father, I'm here. I'm here.

Blood Mountain Villanelle

Where rains are hymns, where waters hum
and haggle, the road leans and heaves,
and engines fail, and work is done.

These mountains, North Georgia's rim,
are heaven enough for me. Up here,
rains are hymns, waters ripple and hum

and hallow the ground. Here the sun
rises late, moss grows on the north side of trees,
engines fail, and work is done.

Ye who are weary come home, come home,
I sang in church when I was a boy. Here I sing
hymns with the rain, here where waters hum.

I sing for myself, I sing for fun
to the birds. I hike and sing along the steep road
where engines fail, where work is done.

Sometimes the birds sing back. They do.
Or not. Who cares? There's peace enough here
where rains become hymns. Where waters hum.
Where engines fail. Where work is done.

The Birds are Dying and Singing

"Milledgeville: A Bird Sanctuary"

—1934 Sign on Washington Street

The local paper reports flocks in Georgia
are dying, no one knows why, their decayed
carcasses inscrutable. Avian scientists
construct improvised morgues, stack trays
on autopsy shelves. Tiny bodies
wait for sanitary disposal.

                                          Meanwhile,
there they go again, our morning birds. One sings
like a rusty hinge. Another whistles, and for fun
I whistle back. Lark, Blue Jay, Finch—
they perch on hidden branches, bird-calls
tuned to a mate's ascendant longing.

Our backyard birds hoot, hackle, or haw, cluck
or coo. They call to each other, not to me or you,
not to the watchers and scribblers who roost
on Washington Street, searching for birdsong.

The watchers hear hinges, whistles, and weeping,
bird-hymns to goldfinch, grosbeak, canary.

Help

It's the end of summer, a Sunday night, 1965. Almost everyone in America is watching The Ed Sullivan Show. "She bought a ticket to ride," the Beatles sing, and the girls on TV are screaming. The camera zooms in, a girl scoops her hands over her cheeks and mouth as if she's about to cry, her beehive hairdo like a helmet over her head.

Aunt Sharon, my mom's baby sister, is seventeen and screaming too. Grandpa smashes his stogie into the ashtray, says he's had enough of this crap, says he's going to bed. Everyone's gone to bed, Aunt Pat, my mom, my baby brother. I'm seven years old, watching my blonde, big-haired aunt scream at the TV, and I'm wondering if I should scream too. Then the screen goes dark, everyone is quiet, and Paul, who Aunt Sharon says she loves the best, sings "Yesterday," and it's true, all my troubles do seem far away. Then the stage lights blaze, the other Beatles return, and the screaming starts all over again.

"Help," the boys sing, "I need somebody," and I know this song, I've heard it on the car radio, my mom tapping her wedding ring in rhythm against the steering wheel. "Help me if you can," Sharon and I sing, "help me get my feet back on the ground." When the song is over, we watch the boys wave goodbye, and then she looks at me.

"You love them, don't you?" she asks, and I say *yes, I love them*.

A year later, Aunt Sharon marries a trucker, *Uncle Jim* to me, my mother says, but his friends all call him *Bunga*. Forty years later, Sharon's kidneys will fail, she will die young, like her mother, brother, and sisters before her. Her skin will turn sallow, her laugh hoarse and hollow. She will hold on as long as she can, her husband, two boys, and her friends from the trailer park close by. My mother, her last living sister, close by. No one's screaming. No one's singing. No one's crying. No one can help her die. Not the good old gals from the neighborhood bar, not her sons all grown up, not even her chain-smoking, big-hearted Bunga.

If only Ed Sullivan could rise from the dead, bring back those boys who made the big girls cry, bring back those black-and-white Sunday nights, when I was so much younger, when Sharon wasn't much older, and all the help we needed was squeezed inside a nineteen-inch Zenith TV, back when all our troubles seemed so far away, when yesterday was only yesterday.

The Day of the Eclipse, My Mother Is Almost Herself Again

The afternoon of the eclipse, sister moon devours brother sun.
Or maybe it's mad Maiden Moon who swallows Father Sun. Or maybe
it's two Chinese dragons squabbling. The day of the eclipse,
radio experts haggle over gods and monsters, eternal
wonders and terrors. I'm driving in the dark, lost
and reliving my morning phone call home.

    "Crazy day," my father says.

His voice sounds far away, and I ask if he and Mother
can hear me. I ask them how they are.

    "Fine," Dad says. "We're here, just fine."
    "We're here," my mother says. "Just fine."

"Remember the Fulton County Fair eclipse,"
I say, "way back in sixty-three?"

    "Nope," my father says, "doesn't ring a bell."
    "Nope, no bells," my mother says.

"We watched the horse and buggy races, the tractor pull.
Aunt Patty told us not to look or we'd go blind.

    "That's right," Dad says. "Now I remember."
    "That's right," Mom says. "I remember now!"

And I want to believe that the light in her eyes might still
ignite, and all at once, she almost sounds like herself again.

    "*Patty loved to laugh*," my mother says. "*She was so skinny,
    winters we cuddled under the covers to keep each other warm.*"

Then my mother stops remembering, so I tell her about the day
the Fulton County Fair went dark, how she and her sister Patty
laid out a blanket for all of us, how we ate bologna
sandwiches, cherry popsicles, and everyone at the fair

waited for the sun to vanish. I tell her how day turned
into night, how I didn't want to look away. How I wanted
to stare into the dark and search the sky
for one last glimmer of light.

The Holy Land

For Susan, 1970-2004

The mud puddle is holy to the sparrow
and to the mud. The empty space
between branches is not empty and is
holy, mid-leap, to the gray squirrel.
The fig tree is holy to the long-tailed monkey.
The town dump is holy to the long-tailed rat.
And the sturdy, narrow branch is holy
to the long tail. The deep water is holy
to the sturgeon and to the sunlight.
The moist soil six inches deep
is holy to the earthworm and to the grass.
Jerusalem is holy to shy beetles crouching
in street corners. The busy road to Mecca is holy
to the hungry crow. Washington dogs galumph with joy
on the holy land of Monument Park.

If Susan were alive, a poet of the world, at home
in Tehran and New York, Geneva, Paris, Amman,
she'd laugh. *Mes petits amis*, she'd say,
watch where you step.

Anno Domini 2004

The large brown spider hunts freely in our crawl space.

A gray squirrel dies beside our road.
On morning walks, I watch its body collapse in the grass.

My wife and I share our woods with a white-tailed doe.
She will birth two fawns, their slender ankles smaller than
my thumb's muscle. One fawn will starve before the year's out.

After a dry spell, hard rains soak the ground.
Come spring, our dogwood tree erupts in red-and-white blossoms.

In another part of the world, something else
falls from the sky. Something else blooms.

This year, so many shapely bodies wither, dangle, or die.
Lord, so many deaths to be added up and numbered.

Commandments

I.

The honeybee's dance
The cicada's siren
Baby Zöe's smile
Are all you need
to know of God.

II.

The noonday sun is not God.
The Ohio cornfield is not God.
The humpback whale is not God.
The Pope, Dalai Lama, and Buddha
Are so bald, so happy.

III.

The President says *God bless America*.
The Ayatollah says *Allah'u Akbar*.
The gully buster Preacher says *Jesus is coming*.
That dark silence that frightens us at night
Is the universe listening, listening, listening.

Come Back

For the first time in my life,
I wake up with a stiff lower back
and a ringing deep inside my ear.

I must have slept wrong, I say
to my wife, as if all my life,
curled up and cozy, I'd known
the right way to sleep.

Turn, she says, *tell me where it hurts.*
Slowly, I roll over to the other side
of the bed, and my wife massages muscles
I could never reach. She whispers to me
in a voice I cannot hear or understand.

Perhaps my left ear, that silly flap
of cartilage, lay folded too long against the pillow.
Perhaps half deaf, I've dreamed middle-aged
half dreams. Perhaps all the muscles in my body
have slipped their sockets.

Lord, one last night before I die, let me sleep
like a baby. Morning, like a man raised from the dead,
let me leap out of bed, button down a ruffled shirt.
Let me stretch, snap my suspenders, let me lean over
and lace up old spats. Let me find the spotlight, have a waltz
with my upright wife. Let me give her a wink, cruise
off stage, then shuffle back for one long, final bow:

My fingers sweep the floor, my left knee
buckles, my ears swell with blood
and applause, then silence, then a faraway bell.

Obituary

Eighty-three years old, June Fox, childless, never
married, a first-grade teacher, retired, flies
from Atlanta to Pittsburgh, headed home
to Rimersburg. The old DC-10, carpet worn
and wings scarred, lurches and dips.

She does not flinch. Head down, hands folded
in her lap, she asks me what my hobbies are.
I like hiking in the mountains, I tell her,
and dancing with my wife. I tell her I like
a good song. Blues. Jazz.

"Can you believe," she says, "I like jazz, too,
a woman my age?" She tells me her heart
is perfect, the doctor told her so, and after
her last exam, she wrote her own obituary.

"Was it hard?" I ask.
"Laughed," she says, "most of the time."

I want to ask her if she'd dance with me
in the aisle, above clouds bouldering in the sky
like Appalachian mountains. Instead,
I ask if she told the whole truth, and she says
yes, nothing but, then confesses scribbling
one hundred years old for the day she'd die.

She wrote goodbye to all her old students—doctors now
and lawyers, nurses, teachers themselves, husbands, wives,
and two men in jail—impossible to name them,
she wrote that she loved them, loved them all.

So listen, you high-flying lovebirds and jailbirds,
no matter your flock or feather, happy,
hapless or hopeless: June Fox loved you all.

A Romance

Friday nights we dance in the kitchen, shimmy
and salsa, or slide in white socks
across the linoleum. My wife pirouettes,
levitates her knee: She cocks her leg, points her big toe
straight down, then kicks her foot into the empty air—
and I think how beautiful she is, how for a moment she overcomes
gravity, how the look in her eyes is so like a ballerina's—

or maybe it's Chuck Connors' look on TV's *The Rifleman*?
I remember those opening credits, the way Chuck
strides down Main Street, how he hugs to his hip
a Winchester rifle. How his jaw was as sharp as Dick Tracy's,
how red-blooded man and Sunday cartoon
were fearless, lipless. Oh, how like a tango

the way stiff-legged Connors blasted through town,
or like a double play, when young Chuck was a Dodger,
jamming steel cleats against the canvas bag (his swivel
and pivot a rookie's pirouette), as he shot the ball
to first, the swift-footed runner out by half a step.

Another Friday night, I'm tipsy and spinning, dancing with my wife
at a friend's wedding. Dipping and kicking up my feet, holding on
for love and most of all for balance, I want to whisper new proposals,
true-blue words from a heart still tender, limber, and beating fast:

Oh Honey, let's go extra innings. Let's turn two. Let's dance
ourselves out of town and into the sunset.

My Wife and I Learn to Accept Our Clutter

Stacks of magazines are a comfort.
Their headlines are like promises.

Dishes pile up in the sink. How lucky
and well-fed my wife and I are.

That litter of bills and credit card offers
must mean our lives are in perfect balance.

Our unmade bed invites us to nap
and make love in the afternoons.

Talking at night on our porch, we notice
how even our sky is cluttered with stars.

Notes

"*Between the Numbers.*" The June 16, 1958 issue of *Life* magazine made this recession era observation about the U.S. economy: "In its first year as a consumer, baby is a potential market for $800 worth of products. And even before returning from the hospital, a new baby represents an outlay of roughly $450 in medical expenses." At $102.35, I was a bargain, according to *Life*.

"*From a Back Alley Balcony in Tuscany, I See Dante's Starlings.*" From my apartment balcony, I watched starlings ("li spiriti mali") fill the sky, just as Dante described them centuries ago (*Inferno*, Canto V, lines 42-44) as a simile for souls whose sin was lust. An idiomatic translation for the last line of the tercet is *no hope can ever comfort them*:

> così quel fiato li spiriti mali
>   di qua, di la, di giù, di sù li mena;
> nulla speranza li conforta...

"*Killing Pigs.*" This poem is dedicated to Donna Deason, a longtime employee of Georgia College, in Milledgeville, who lived to see this poem published in *Chelsea*, to her delight, but who tragically succumbed to cancer before the publication of this book.

"*Lost Lesson from Japanese Children's Class in Shushin.*" For an ambivalent modern context related to extreme lessons in *shushin* that Omasu's story used to represent to earlier generations, see the *New York Times*, August 4, 1997:

"In the old days we had shushin to teach us filial piety," said Masae Minami, 86, the matriarch of a family that runs a clothing store in Omiya. "But now that's all gone. I think the old system was better, because society has become very chaotic. Now it's as if you can do anything you like to parents."

"*Sestina Qué Triste*" is dedicated to Winston McCloud, our neighbor on the black sand beach north of Cahuita, Costa Rica, and to whom my wife and I will always be grateful.

"*In Cortona, Walking Beside a Wall Erected Before Christ, I Contemplate Longing.*" See Dante's *Inferno* (Canto IV, line 42): "che sanza spema vivemo in diseo" ("who without hope, live in desire"). In Cortona, Italy, you can witness this wall for yourself.

"*Poetry Fathers.*" This poem was inspired by a real dinner I attended in Macon with Louis Simpson and his hosts (Simpson was visiting for a month in Georgia as the Distinguished Ferrol Sams Chair at Mercer University). Simpson's role in this poem reflects actual conversations over dinner; other poets (including Donald Hall and Robert Bly, who I first met in 1980 at the end of my senior year in college) appear in this poem only as I imagine and with all appropriate reverence for the living and the dead.

"*What Goats Know.*" I *did* gaze at, but did not climb "Ha Ling Peak" in Alberta, Canada.

"*The Holy Land.*" This poem is dedicated to Susan Atefat-Peckham (1970-2004) *in memoriam*: Poet and citizen of the world, Susan's soul departed this earth too soon.

"*Obituary.*" I sat beside June Fox on a 1998 flight from Atlanta to Pittsburgh. As I write these notes in the summer of 2019, I'd like to hope that, somewhere in Rimersburg, Pennsylvania, June Fox is listening to jazz, kicking up her heels, and celebrating her 104th birthday.

Acknowledgements

I would like to thank the following publications in which poems or original versions of poems were first published:

The Atlanta Review	"How Like a Son"
Chelsea	"Killing Pigs" "Poetry Fathers"
The Connecticut Review	"A Romance"
Connotation Press	"Sestina Qué Triste"
Dos Passos Review	"Between the Numbers"
The Gettysburg Review	"Lost Lesson from Japanese Children's Class on *Shushin*"
Great River Review	"The Birds are Dying and Singing" "From a Back Alley Balcony in Tuscany, I See Dante's Starlings"
Luna	"The Bird I Would Be" "Searching for Emus"
Margie Review	"Commandments"
Mid-American Review	"Back Roads"
The Mississippi Review	"The Holy Land"
Nightsun	"1969" "Feeding Pigs"
Rivendell	"Blood Mountain Villanelle"
Poet Lore	"Bird Offering" "A Fable: Why the Village Will Never Be Empty"

The Southeast Review (Formerly *Sundog*)	"Obituary"
The Southern Review	"My Wife and I Learn to Accept Our Clutter" "Anno Domini 2004" "My Sister Tells Me Her Prayer for the *World of Men*"
The Tusculum Review	"In Cortona, Walking Beside a Wall Erected Before Christ, I Contemplate Longing"
West Branch	"The Only Other Beautiful Thing"

Martin **Lammon**'s first book of poems, *News From Where I Live*, won the Arkansas Poetry Award and was published by the University of Arkansas Press. He also edited the book *Written in Water, Written in Stone: Twenty Years of Poets on Poetry* for the University of Michigan Press's "Poets on Poetry" series, an anthology of essays and interviews from the series under the general editorship of distinguished poet Donald Hall (U.S. Poet Laureate, 2006-2007). Lammon has taught at several colleges and universities in Ohio, Connecticut, Pennsylvania, and West Virginia, but in 1997 he landed at Georgia College in Milledgeville, where he was the Fuller E. Callaway endowed Flannery O'Connor Chair in Creative Writing from 1997-2018. There, he founded the university's MFA program in 2001-2002, which 10 years later was listed as one of the nation's "Top 25 Underrated Creative Writing MFA Programs (2011-2012)" in *The Huffington Post* (spring 2011). He has founded two national literary journals (*Kestrel* at Fairmont State in West Virginia; *Arts & Letters* at Georgia College) and served on local, state, and national arts boards, including two terms (2000-2002) as President of the Association of Writers and Writing Programs (AWP) the nation's largest professional association of writers, editors, teachers and students of creative writing. He has conducted dozens of workshops across the country and abroad for young writers (K-12) at public schools, libraries, and special summer programs, as well as community programs for older writers and lovers of literature. He has also been an active fundraiser and advocate for literary and cultural programs, professional opportunities for writers, and student scholarships.

Lammon's poems and essays have appeared in such literary journals as *The Atlanta Review, Chattahoochee Review, Gettysburg Review, The Iowa Review, Nimrod* (for three poems awarded a Hardman/Pablo Neruda Prize by Pulitzer Prize-winning poet W.S. Merwin), *Ploughshares, Poet Lore, Poets & Writers, The Southern Review,* and *Zone 3* ("The Body Electric," about living in Costa Rica, was listed among "Notable Essays of 2008" in *Best American Essays*). Born, raised, and educated in Ohio, Lammon has also lived in Connecticut, Pennsylvania, West Virginia, and Costa Rica, before moving to Georgia in 1997. After many years teaching and living in Milledgeville, he now resides in Atlanta where he continues his work as a writer and an advocate locally and nationally for writers and the literary arts.

www.ingramcontent.com/pod-product-compliance
Lightning Source LLC
Chambersburg PA
CBHW020254090426
42735CB00010B/1924